T0086894

THE OXFORD PIANO METHOI

PIANO TIME OPERA

arranged by

Pauline Hall

MUSIC DEPARTMENT

OXFORD
UNIVERSITY PRESS

Oxford University Press, Great Clarendon Street, Oxford OX2 6DP, England
Oxford University Press Inc., 198 Madison Avenue, New York, NY 10016, USA

© Oxford University Press 1998

All rights reserved. No part of this publication may be reproduced, stored in a retrieval system, or transmitted, in any form or by any means, without the prior permission in writing of Oxford University Press.

Permission to perform the works in this anthology in public should normally be obtained from the Performing Right Society Ltd. (PRS), 29/33 Berners Street, London W1P 4AA, or its affiliated Societies in each country throughout the world, unless the owner or the occupier of the premises being used holds a licence from the Society.

Permission to make a recording must be obtained in advance from the Mechanical Copyright Protection Society Ltd. (MCPS), Elgar House, 41 Streatham High Road, London SW16 1ER, or its affiliated Societies in each country throughout the world.

Illustrations by John Taylor

Operas contain some of the most beautiful and memorable tunes ever written, and we've all probably caught ourselves humming or singing one of these famous melodies at some time or other. Well, now you can experience the thrill and fun of the opera house from your own piano stool with this selection of really easy graded arrangements of well-known arias and choruses. You could perform your favourite pieces to friends or family, but beware, they may want to sing along!

P.H.

CONTENTS

Arietta from *Romeo and Juliet* GOUNOD 5
'Libiamo' from *La Traviata* VERDI 6
'Dove sono' from *The Marriage of Figaro* MOZART 7
'One fine day' from *Madame Butterfly* PUCCINI 8
Overture from *The Barber of Seville* ROSSINI 9
Waltz from *Eugene Onegin* TCHAIKOVSKY 10
'Là ci darem la mano' from *Don Giovanni* MOZART 11
'O mio babbino caro' from *Gianni Schicchi* PUCCINI 12
'The flowers that bloom in the Spring' from *The Mikado* SULLIVAN 13
Dance from *The Bartered Bride* SMETANA 14
Gavotte from *Iphigenia in Aulis* GLUCK 15
Chorus of wedding guests from *Lucia di Lammermoor* DONIZETTI 16
'Bei Männern' from *The Magic Flute* MOZART 17
Gavotte from *The Gondoliers* SULLIVAN 18
Pilgrim's chorus from *Tannhäuser* WAGNER 19
Laughing song from *Die Fledermaus* STRAUSS 20
March from *Rinaldo* HANDEL 22
'My heart was so free' from *The Beggar's Opera* PEPUSCH 23
Minuet from *Berenice* HANDEL 24
Prayer from *Der Freischütz* WEBER 25
'Voi che sapete' from *The Marriage of Figaro* MOZART 26
Barcarolle from *Tales of Hoffmann* OFFENBACH 28
'Where'er you walk' from *Semele* HANDEL 29
Chorus of the Hebrew slaves from *Nabucco* VERDI 30
Bird-catcher's song from *The Magic Flute* MOZART 31
'Fairest Isle' from *King Arthur* PURCELL 32
Intermezzo from *Cavalleria Rusticana* MASCAGNI 33
Soldiers' chorus from *Faust* GOUNOD 34
Habanera from *Carmen* BIZET 36
'Brother come and dance with me' from *Hansel and Gretel* HUMPERDINCK 38
Flower duet from *Lakmé* DELIBES 39

Arietta from Romeo and Juliet

Charles Gounod is best known for his *Ave Maria*, composed on top of J. S. Bach's famous Prelude in C. This well-known waltz comes from the opera Gounod composed in 1867.

Charles Gounod (1818–93)

Moderato

mp

mf

© Oxford University Press 1998

Printed in Great Britain
OXFORD UNIVERSITY PRESS, MUSIC DEPARTMENT, GREAT CLARENDON STREET, OXFORD OX2 6DP

Photocopying this copyright material is ILLEGAL.

'Libiamo' from La Traviata

La Traviata has always been the most popular of Verdi's twenty-nine operas because of its many memorable tunes. At its first performance the audience erupted into laughter when the 'fragile' heroine turned out to be an enormous soprano! This piece is a jovial drinking song.

Giuseppe Verdi (1813–1901)

'Dove sono' from The Marriage of Figaro

The Marriage of Figaro was a failure when first performed in 1786, and closed after only nine performances. Since then it has established itself as one of Mozart's greatest works. This gracious piece is sung by the Countess, who laments that her husband, the Count, no longer loves her.

Wolfgang Amadeus Mozart (1756–91)

Andante

mp

'One fine day' from Madame Butterfly

Madame Butterfly is set in Japan. It tells the tragic story of an American naval Lieutenant who falls in love with a beautiful young Japanese girl, only to leave her and return with a new American wife.

Giacomo Puccini (1858–1924)

© CASA RICORDI—BMG RICORDI S.p.A. Milan. Reproduced by arrangement

Overture from The Barber of Seville

The Barber of Seville, possibly the best-loved Italian comic opera, tells the story of the rascally barber Figaro. Rossini completed an average of two operas a year for nineteen years and this opera was written in just under two weeks.

Gioacchino Rossini (1792–1868)

Allegro vivace

p *mf* *p* *mf* *f*

Waltz from Eugene Onegin

This famous waltz comes from the scene of a glittering ball celebrating the birthday of Tatyana, the heroine of the story, who has fallen hopelessly in love with Eugene Onegin.

Pyotr Ilyich Tchaikovsky (1840–93)

'Là ci darem la mano' from Don Giovanni

Don Giovanni has been generally accepted as Mozart's greatest opera. This tender love song is sung as a duet between the Don and his latest sweetheart, who unfortunately happens to be engaged to another man.

Wolfgang Amadeus Mozart (1756–91)

Andante

'O mio babbino caro' from Gianni Schicchi

Gianni Schicchi is a comic opera set in medieval Florence. This well-known aria is sung by the heroine Lauretta, as she pleads with her father to let her marry the man she loves.

Giacomo Puccini (1858–1924)

© CASA RICORDI—BMG RICORDI S.p.A. Milan. Reproduced by arrangement

'The flowers that bloom in the Spring' from The Mikado

Sir Arthur Sullivan collaborated with W. S. Gilbert to produce a series of operas. Although the pair frequently quarrelled, the combination of Gilbert's witty words and Sullivan's tuneful music made their operas terrifically popular in Victorian England.

Sir Arthur Sullivan (1842–1900)

Dance from The Bartered Bride

Smetana lived and worked in Prague. He loved Czech folk music, and used some of its lilting melodies and rustic dances in his own works. *The Bartered Bride* is an opera about a peasant girl whose parents want her to marry the village simpleton.

Bedrich Smetana (1824–84)

Moderato

mf

sempre stacc.

f

Gavotte from Iphigenia in Aulis

A gavotte is a stately, graceful dance in quadruple time. Gluck's opera is based on an ancient Greek drama, in which King Agamemnon decides to sacrifice his daughter Iphigenia to appease the Goddess Diana. Luckily for Iphigenia, his plans are thwarted.

Christoph Gluck (1714–87)

Grazioso

Chorus of wedding guests from Lucia di Lammermoor

Lucia di Lammermoor was Donizetti's most successful opera. It is a tragedy set in 16th-century Scotland and contains a famous scene where the heroine goes mad. Sadly, Donizetti himself went mad in real life and spent his last years in an asylum.

Gaetano Donizetti (1797–1848)

'Bei Männern' from The Magic Flute

The Magic Flute was written in the last year of Mozart's life. The fairytale plot was very popular with the Viennese audience, with its colourful cast of a magician, a prince and princess, priests, a bird-catcher, a serpent, the Queen of the Night, and magic bells and flute.

Wolfgang Amadeus Mozart (1756–91)

Moderato

p

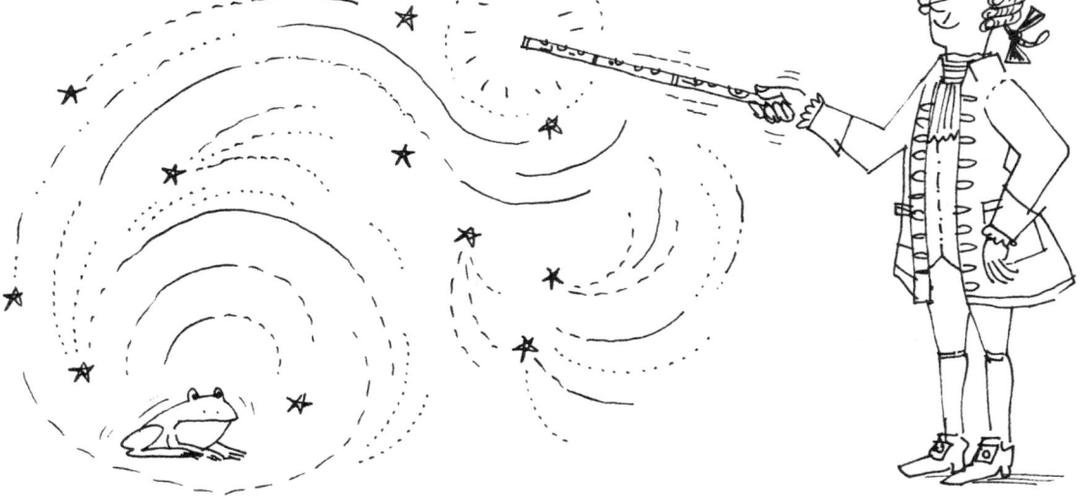

Gavotte from The Gondoliers

Here, the two gondolier brothers, who have just learned that they are to be kings, are being instructed in the noble art of dancing—with mixed success!

Sir Arthur Sullivan (1842–1900)

Tempo di gavotta

mf

Pilgrims' chorus from Tannhäuser

This chorus is sung by a procession of pilgrims returning from Rome. It appears in the opera's third act, and builds to a tremendous climax, but is best known from the orchestral overture, which is often performed separately.

Richard Wagner (1813–83)

Laughing song from Die Fledermaus

Die Fledermaus ('The Bat') is a comic opera set in 19th-century Vienna. The plot revolves around the mistaken identities and misunderstandings of the main characters attending a fancy dress ball, one of whom is disguised as a bat!

Johann Strauss (1825–99)

4
2
1
p
5
3
4

March from Rinaldo

German by birth, Handel lived most of his life in England. This was the first opera he wrote there, and a great success. Rinaldo was leader of the crusaders, and this march was later adopted by the Life Guards regiment as their regimental tune.

George Frideric Handel (1685–1759)

Moderato

'My heart was so free' from The Beggar's Opera

The characters in *The Beggar's Opera* are a motley crew of thieves, highwaymen, and pick-pockets. The plot is set in the London underworld of the eighteenth century, and the tunes are mostly a collection of the 'pop' songs of the day.

John Christopher Pepusch (1667–1752)

Moderato

Minuet from Berenice

There have been over twenty operas composed on the story of Berenice. Apart from this beautiful and much-loved minuet, the remainder of Handel's opera is, sadly, rarely performed.

George Frideric Handel (1685–1759)

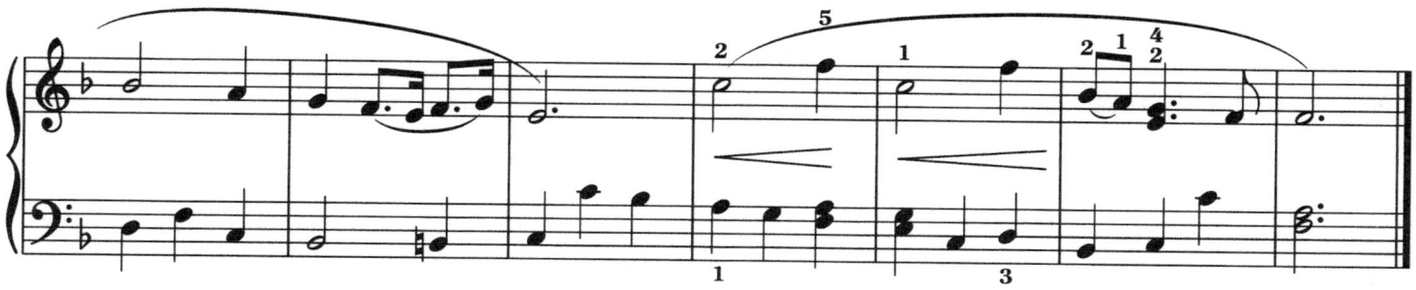

Prayer from Der Freischütz

The heroine, Agathe, prays for protection on waking from an ominous dream. Her fiancé, Max, has made a pact with an evil spirit, in return for seven magic bullets to win a shooting contest.

Carl Maria von Weber (1786–1826)

Andante

p

'Voi che sapete' from The Marriage of Figaro

The central character is the same Figaro who is portrayed in Rossini's *Barber of Seville.* The plot is a complicated one, full of characters in disguise, tricks, and misunderstandings. However, all ends happily.

Wolfgang Amadeus Mozart (1756–91)

a tempo

p

Barcarolle from Tales of Hoffmann

A barcarolle is a type of boating song that is supposed to have originated from the songs of the Venetian gondoliers. The gently rocking 6/8 rhythm imitates the motion of a gondola, or small boat.

Jacques Offenbach (1819–80)

'Where'er you walk' from Semele

Although *Semele*, like many of Handel's operas, is not often performed, this particular aria is quite well-known. It demonstrates his great gift for beautiful melodies.

George Frideric Handel (1685–1759)

Andante

p

mf

Chorus of the Hebrew slaves from Nabucco

During his long life, Verdi became the most popular Italian opera composer, a member of parliament, and a national hero. This opera uses the story of Nebuchadnezzar, the Babylonian king who captured Jerusalem and took the Hebrews into captivity.

Giuseppe Verdi (1813–1901)

Bird-catcher's song from The Magic Flute

The bird-catcher is a character called Papageno, who charms the birds with tunes from his pipe. In this song he merrily sings that he'd rather catch girls than birds!

Wolfgang Amadeus Mozart (1756–91)

Allegretto

mf

pp

mf

pp

f

'Fairest Isle' from King Arthur

Henry Purcell was a choirboy in the Royal Chapel. 'Fairest Isle' has been described as his most perfect song: play it and see!

Henry Purcell (*c.*1659–95)

Intermezzo from Cavalleria Rusticana

An intermezzo is a short instrumental piece played between the acts of an opera. This one comes from Mascagni's first opera, written for a competition in which it won first prize and great acclaim throughout Italy.

Pietro Mascagni (1863–1945)

© Warner Chappell Music Ltd., London W1Y 3FA. Reprinted by permission of International Music Publications Ltd.

Soldiers' chorus from Faust

Gounod's *Faust* must rank as one of the world's most popular operas. It was a particular favourite of Queen Victoria, who asked to have part of it sung to her just before her death.

Charles Gounod (1818–93)

f
ff

Habanera from Carmen

Bizet's *Carmen* is one of the world's most popular operas. It tells the story of the gypsy girl Carmen and her rival lovers, a soldier and a toreador (bullfighter). A habanera is a slow, sensuous dance, which was the forerunner of the tango.

Georges Bizet (1838–75)

'Brother come and dance with me' from Hansel and Gretel

Humperdinck was a friend of Wagner. Only after Wagner's death did he feel confident enough in his own music to begin work on this, his most famous opera. Here, Hansel complains that he doesn't know how to dance, so Gretel teaches him.

Engelbert Humperdinck (1854–1921)

mf

p

mf

cresc.

f

Flower duet from Lakmé

Lakmé is set in India in the mid-nineteenth century, and tells of the doomed love affair of a British officer and the daughter of a Hindu Priest. Delibes was a French composer. *Lakmé* is the only one of his operas still regularly performed, and he is now better known for his ballet music.

Léo Delibes (1836–91)

Andante cantabile

mp

1.

2.

mf

cresc.

f

sub. p

mp

rall.

Reproduced and printed by
Halstan & Co. Ltd., Amersham, Bucks., England